DATE DUE

AP 6'91			
MY 23 91			
JY 2 '93			
APR 19 '94			
MAY 2 '94			
AUG 14 94			
MR 25 13			
10-22-94			

YESTERDAY'S TRUCKS

No.45

GMC

PATRICK C. DORIN

Lerner Publications Company • Minneapolis, Minnesota

LIBRARY OF CONGRESS CATALOGING IN PUBLICATION DATA

Dorin, Patrick C.
  Yesterday's trucks.

  (Superwheels & thrill sports)
  SUMMARY: Describes the various kinds of
trucks produced between 1900 and the 1940s
and mentions the hobby of collecting and
restoring old trucks.
  1. Trucks—History—Juvenile literature.
[1. Trucks—History] I. Title. II. Series
TL230.D67   629.2′24′0904   81-20717
ISBN 0-8225-0502-9   AACR2

Manufactured in the United States of America

International Standard Book Number: 0-8225-0502-9
Library of Congress Catalog Card Number: 81-20717

  2 3 4 5 6 7 8 9 10 90 89 87 86 85 84 83

CONTENTS

INTRODUCTION

For hundreds of years, human beings had to rely on horses or horse-drawn vehicles for transportation over land. During all this time, people probably dreamed of having vehicles that could move under their own power. It was not until around 1600, however, that the first attempts were made to build a self-powered wagon. At that time, some clever Dutch inventors made wagons with sails attached. Since these wagons moved only when the wind was blowing, they weren't very practical. During the early 1700s, Swiss and French inventors tried building wagons that were powered by giant clock springs. They didn't work very well either.

Then in 1769, a French military officer, Captain Nicholas Joseph Cugnot, built a three-wheeled vehicle powered by a steam engine.

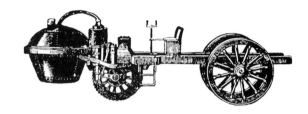

Captain Nicholas Joseph Cugnot's steam-powered vehicle was built in 1769.

Cugnot's clumsy steamer, which could travel no faster than three miles an hour, was the first true ancestor of today's automobiles and trucks. During the late 1700s, many people began building steam-powered vehicles that were used for various purposes. By 1800, buses powered by steam engines were running on the streets of Paris. During this same period, inventors were developing steam-powered locomotives that would soon be used on the world's first railroads.

Americans began building steam-powered wagons as early as 1800. It was not until

In the United States, the first successful steamer made its appearance in 1850.

1850, however, that any of the steamers proved successful. In that year, Richard Dugeon of New York constructed a steam-powered wagon that kept working for 10 whole years.

In the last part of the 1800s, rivals to steam power appeared on the scene. The most important was the gasoline-powered internal combustion engine. Another kind of engine developed at this time worked on the electricity stored in batteries. Vehicles built during this period could use any one of these power sources. Early automobiles, which began to appear in the 1880s, were powered by gasoline, electricity, and steam. The first real trucks also used all three kinds of power.

Trucks were being built in the United States at the very end of the 1800s. In 1896, the Cruickshank Engineering Works of Providence, Rhode Island, converted a horse-drawn van into a steam-powered delivery truck for a local department store. In that same year, the Langert Company of Philadelphia entered a gasoline-powered delivery truck in a race held in New York.

Most of the early trucks were built for delivery service, and quite a few of them were powered by electricity. Some of these electric trucks were quite efficient, especially when compared to the early gasoline-powered trucks.

This early electric truck carried its batteries in a storage compartment between the wheels.

For example, an electric truck had three times the life span of the gasoline model. The electric truck also needed much less care and maintenance because it had 1,000 fewer working parts than a truck with a gasoline engine. Despite its efficiency, however, the electric truck had one big problem—it couldn't travel very far without having its batteries recharged. The batteries were also very heavy, often weighing as much as 1,000 pounds. Because of these disadvantages, the electric truck had all but disappeared from the streets by 1930.

In 1900, the White Company built this steam-powered truck to deliver the sewing machines it manufactured. In later years, White got out of the sewing-machine business and concentrated on building trucks of all kinds.

Steam-powered trucks were also very popular in the early 1900s, but they too had disadvantages. In order to produce steam, these vehicles burned fuel that heated water in a boiler. Depending on their design, steam engines burned either coal, coke, kerosene, or gasoline. Because the fuel had to be fed constantly into the burner, a steam truck had to carry a large supply just to keep the engine going. For example, a coal-burning steam truck had to haul a heavy load of coal, plus the water needed for the boiler. The more fuel and water it carried, the heavier the load and the less room there was for cargo.

Over the long run, neither the steamer nor the electric truck could compete with trucks using gasoline engines. A gasoline-powered truck did not have to carry as heavy a load of fuel as the steamer, and it could make longer journeys than a truck with an electric engine.

It was not long before people realized that trucks with gasoline engines could be counted on to do the job. In order to prove the point, early trucking companies arranged many special tours to show the public just how reliable trucks were. On these tours, groups of trucks made long trips carrying loads of freight. The first cross-country trip made by a truck took place as early as 1911. Six years later, trucks were put to a real test when they were used to carry troops and supplies during World War I. After the war, everyone realized that trucks had an important place on American roads.

One of the biggest problems faced by the early trucking industry was the terrible condition of those roads. There were very few hard-surfaced highways in the United States before 1920. In bad weather, dirt roads turned into rivers of mud, and trucks often spent more time stuck in one place than they did on the move. Other problems were caused by bridges that were not strong enough to support the heavy loads the new trucks carried. It was not until the 1920s that various states began to build the kinds of roads and bridges that were suited to truck traffic.

In 1916, this truck traveled from Seattle to New York carrying a load of Carnation evaporated milk. The truck was supposed to cover the 3,640 miles in 30 days, but the trip actually took twice that long.

During the 1920s, American trucks became bigger, faster, and more specialized. Most of the early trucks had been designed for delivery service, but now the trucking industry was building dump trucks, tank trucks, mail trucks, garbage trucks, and many other varieties.

This Packard moving van was one of the specialized kinds of trucks built during the 1920s.

The Merchants Express, a Dodge delivery truck from 1929, kept the boxy look of earlier American trucks.

Despite their specialized uses, most of these new trucks kept the boxy look of the earlier trucks. It was not until the mid-1940s that truck design became more streamlined, with smoother lines and rounded corners. The trucks built during the 1940s and 1950s were the predecessors of the sleek tankers and huge 18-wheelers that can be seen on the highways today.

Modern tank trucks are much bigger and more streamlined than this little oil tanker built in 1931.

This book is not about the large, powerful trucks of the 1980s but about yesterday's trucks, particularly those built between 1900 and 1940. These old trucks are part of a fascinating period of American life that has not been forgotten.

Eighteen-wheelers like this Peterbilt model are powerful trucks that carry heavy loads over today's highways.

These trucks delivered ice cream in the city of Seattle during the early 1900s.

DELIVERY TRUCKS

The very first trucks built in the early 1900s were designed to carry groceries, furniture, and other goods from stores and shops to people's homes. The new trucks also took freight brought by train from railroad stations to customers in towns and cities. These trucks were used only for local delivery service and were never taken out on the highway.

The first delivery trucks looked a lot like horse-drawn wagons—without the horses.

Both the drivers and the cargos of early delivery trucks sat out in the open, with no protection from wind and rain.

A Dodge pick-up from 1919

PICK-UP TRUCKS

The first pick-up trucks were designed for use by people who needed a small truck for general hauling purposes. These little trucks were ideal, especially for farmers, who could use them for many different jobs on the farm. A pick-up could also be driven to town to

When this beautiful pick-up truck was built in the early 1920s, the flapper-style dress worn by the model was all the rage.

pick up supplies and bring them back to the farm.

The pick-up truck first became popular between 1915 and 1920. An early pick-up usually had a small body with an enclosed cab for the driver and one or two passengers. A box-like carrier was mounted over the rear wheels to hold cargo. Like delivery trucks, these first pick-ups looked a lot like the wagons they often replaced. In later designs, the cabs became very boxy in shape. After World War II, pick-ups were designed to look more like automobiles.

These two pick-up trucks from the 1930s show the automobile-influenced styling that was beginning to be popular during this period.

Today pick-ups like this handsome two-toned Chevy are seen on streets and highways all over the United States.

The pick-up truck has turned out to be one of the most popular kinds of trucks ever built. Today pick-ups are owned by all kinds of people in all parts of the United States. The little trucks are used in more ways than could be listed in this short book.

This 1910 dump truck was used to deliver loads of coal.

An Oregon road crew unloading paving material from a dump truck in 1920

DUMP TRUCKS

The dump truck made its first appearance around 1905. Mack Trucks and Pierce Arrow, maker of the famous Pierce Arrow automobile, were two of the first companies to build these trucks.

Dump trucks were very practical vehicles. A dump truck could be used to transport loose, heavy materials such as sand, gravel, coal, or coke. When the truck arrived at its destination, the body could simply be raised

This 1928 Brockway dump truck was unusual because it tilted to the side. Most early dump trucks dumped their loads out the back, like the 1912 Avery shown on the opposite page.

up and tilted, and the load would slide out.

The early dump trucks could carry about a ton of material. By 1910, however, some trucks were designed to handle loads of 3 or 4 tons. Today most dump trucks can carry as much as 40 tons. A modern dump truck used in mining operations can carry loads even heavier.

In the 1920s and 1930s, dump trucks were used to deliver coal to millions of homes throughout the United States. They also carried materials for road building and for countless other jobs.

A tractor trailer speeds down a highway in 1926.

The earliest trailers were not pulled by tractors but by full-size trucks. Because the load-carrying space was doubled, such units were called double bottoms.

TRACTOR TRAILERS

The very first trucks were designed as one unit, with the cab and the load-carrying element joined together. It was not long, however, before trucks with two separate parts appeared on the scene. The front part, called the *tractor,* contained the engines and provided the power that pulled the cargo-carrying part, called the *trailer.* This kind of truck is usually known as a *tractor trailer.*

Trucks with trailers first appeared around 1910, but many of them were not real tractor trailers. Instead they were full-size, single-unit trucks with trailers attached to the rear by a coupling device. The use of a trailer doubled

This 1914 Fruehauf lumber truck was one of the first tractor-trailer models built in the United States.

the truck's cargo-carrying capacity, but it wasn't a very practical arrangement. In 1914, a company called Fruehauf began building trailers that were pulled, not by a truck, but by a modified Model T Ford automobile.

During World War I, real tractor-trailer combinations were used by the American army.

The tractor consisted of a cab with an extension on the back that was supported by a set of wheels. The trailer unit, which fastened onto this extension, had full-size wheels only in the rear. Its front wheels were very small and were used only to support the trailer when it was not attached to the tractor. These wheels

Today's huge semis have the same arrangement of wheels as the early tractor trailers.

could be raised or lowered by a crank on the side of the trailer. Most modern trailers have the same arrangement of wheels; they are usually called *semi-trailers* because they have only half as many riding wheels as a full trailer. Often the name for such a unit is shortened to *semi,* pronounced SEM-eye.

The early trailers were simply boxes on wheels, and they were used in much the same way as railroad boxcars. By the mid-1920s, however, trailers were being designed to haul special cargos. Some tractor-trailer units carried milk, butter, and other foods in trailers that could be loaded with ice to keep the contents

This refrigerated trailer from the 1920s carried cans of milk from the train station to the plant where the milk was processed.

from spoiling in hot weather. By the 1930s, livestock trailers were in use. A livestock trailer was built like a railroad cattle car, with slats or openings in the sides that made a kind of cage for the animals being hauled. This design gave cattle and hogs plenty of light and fresh air while they were on the way to their destination.

In the period after World War II, tractor trailers got bigger and bigger. Today some of them are capable of carrying 40 tons of freight! These big trucks are probably the most important cargo haulers on modern highways.

A Mack tank truck built around 1915

TANK TRUCKS

Tank trucks, or tankers, were invented to carry liquid cargo, especially gasoline and other oil products. In the early 1900s, when tank trucks first appeared, vehicles powered by gasoline engines were becoming more and more common. Some kind of carrier was

A 1920 International Harvester oil tanker

needed to deliver gasoline to service stations and other suppliers. The tanker was just the right truck to do the job.

Early tankers came in all shapes and sizes. Some had tanks shaped like boxes, while others carried their cargos in cylinder-shaped tanks. The cylinder turned out to be a better design, and it is still in use today.

Tank trucks like this 1928 White were also used as street-cleaning units.

This White tanker from 1930 was used to transport fuel at an airport.

Tank trucks were originally used to carry oil and gasoline, but other jobs were soon found for them. Some tankers were used to bring drinking water to crews working in desert areas. Others carried oil that was sprayed on dusty roads in the days before paved roads were common. People discovered that tankers could carry many kinds of liquids, including milk, acids, and thick syrups. The only requirement was that the liquid could be released from the tank simply by turning a kind of faucet or valve.

The first tank trucks were built in one piece, with the cab and the tank joined together. By the mid-1920s, however, many tankers were designed as tractor trailers. This change in design made it possible to use bigger tanks and to carry much heavier loads. Today's tankers look very different from the tank trucks of the early 1900s.

A mail truck from the early 1900s loaded with bags of mail

MAIL TRUCKS

The United States Postal Service began using trucks before almost anybody else had even thought of the idea. In fact, the postal service was using small three-wheeled trucks before 1900 to carry mail in certain cities. By 1910, modified delivery trucks hauled mail within cities and towns. Cross-country mail service was provided by trains in this period.

In 1914, this elegant little truck delivered packages for the United States Postal Service.

In the mid-1920s, airmail service began in the United States, and trucks traveled to and from airports to pick up and deliver mail.

Today airplanes carry most mail between American cities, but trucks are still an important part of local postal delivery systems.

LOGGING TRUCKS

Trucks did not go to work in the woods until about 1915. Up to this time, horses were usually used to haul logs to the nearest rail-road. As the logging industry grew, however, the distances between the logging sites and the railroad tracks became too great for horses

A logging truck on a steep mountain road

to cover. The only solution to the problem was to use trucks.

Many different kinds of trucks were built for the logging industry. Loggers used ordinary single-unit trucks for small loads, but large tractor trailers were needed to haul long, heavy logs. Some big logs might be as much as five or six feet thick. It was quite a job to drive a truck pulling such a heavy load.

Since World War II, logging trucks have become much bigger and much safer to drive. The brake systems on modern trucks are far better than they were on trucks used in the 1920s. Nevertheless, it still takes a brave and careful driver to handle a heavy logging truck on a steep, winding mountain road.

These Mack trucks hauled supplies for the United States Army during World War I.

OTHER KINDS OF TRUCKS

Many different kinds of trucks were used in the United States during the years between 1900 and 1940. There were fire trucks, cement trucks, police department trucks, and garbage trucks, just to name a few. Still other trucks were designed for use by the United States

This speedy truck carried fire-fighting equipment in a small Iowa town during the 1930s.

military forces. These trucks not only hauled supplies but also carried large numbers of soldiers from place to place. All of these kinds of trucks are still used today, even though their designs may have changed and their sizes and carrying capacities are usually much bigger.

Trucks used by the Indianapolis Police Department in the early 1900s

Cement-mixing trucks were first used around 1916.

Built in 1917, this unusual International Harvester dump truck has been restored to its original condition.

ENJOYING YESTERDAY'S TRUCKS

Although most of the trucks built between 1900 and 1940 are no longer in use, you can still enjoy seeing them and learning about them. Many organizations and individuals collect and restore old trucks. Museums like the Smithsonian in Washington, D.C., have old trucks on display so that people can study them and learn something about the history of trucking in the United States. The National Transportation Museum in St. Louis, Missouri, also has many early trucks in its collection, as well as old-time buses and railroad equipment.

Other old trucks have been preserved by companies or individuals. In many cases, these trucks have been fixed up and run just as well as they did when they were new. Of course, such trucks are not used for hauling freight. Instead they are brought out for parades, company picnics, and other festivities. Sometimes people are given a chance to ride in a truck that may be as much as 60 years old. On such occasions, yesterday's trucks often become the hit of the day.

Another way to learn about old trucks is to become a member of the American Truck Historical Society. This organization, which has its offices in Birmingham, Alabama, has done a great deal of work in collecting and preserving information related to the history of trucks and trucking. The society has a large collection of books, magazines, and

A construction company is the proud owner of this restored dump truck.

A 1941 tractor on display without the automobile carrier that it originally pulled

photographs that can be used for research by people interested in yesterday's trucks.

Anyone can join the American Truck Historical Society. Members receive a magazine that contains many articles and pictures about the history of trucking and also about the modern trucking industry. A member can also attend chapter meetings and national

Before restoration, this 1937 Mack truck was in bad shape, but after weeks of hard work, the engine ran just as smoothly as it did when it was new.

conventions of the society, where people who share an interest in trucks get together to talk about their favorite subject. If you would like to know more about the society, you can write to:

American Truck Historical Society
201 Office Park Drive
Birmingham, Alabama 35223

One of the best ways to learn about yesterday's trucks is by collecting and working on them yourself. Restoring an old-time truck is hard work, but it can also be great fun. If you are lucky, someday you might be able to enjoy this fascinating hobby. Fixing up a rusty old truck until it looks just like new is not only fun but it is also a good way to make sure that the trucks of the past will still be around for many years to come.

A 1926 dump truck ready to take part in a parade

ACKNOWLEDGEMENTS: The author wishes to thank Joseph Salisbury, Superior Publishing Company, Seattle, Washington, Robert F. Karolevitz, and Zoe S. James, Executive Director, American Truck Historical Society, for their assistance and for the following photographs from the Robert F. Karolevitz Collection: pp. 3, 5; p. 4, Smithsonian Institution; pp. 6 (White Motor Corporation), 15, 41 (General Motors Corporation), Automobile Manufacturers Association, Inc.; p. 8, Seattle Chamber of Commerce; pp. 13, 37, Kenworth Motor Truck Company; p. 14, American Trucking Association, Inc.; pp. 22, 26, General Motors Corporation; p. 23, Oregon State Highway Department; p. 24, Brockway Motor Trucks; p. 27, Fruehauf Corporation; p. 30, United States Department of Agriculture; p. 31, Mack Trucks, Inc.; pp. 35, 43, International Harvester Company; p. 36, United States Post Office Department; p. 38, Special Collections Division, Suzzallo Library, University of Washington; p. 42, Washington State Department of Highways. Additional photographs reproduced through the courtesy of: pp. 9, 16, 17, 25, 46, American Truck Historical Society; pp. 10, 11, 18, 19, 20, Chrysler Corporation; p. 12, Peterbilt Motors Company; p. 21, Chevrolet Public Relations; p. 28, Fruehauf Corporation; pp. 29, 44, 45, 47, Patrick C. Dorin; p. 32, Merrill Transport Company; pp. 33, 34, White Motor Corporation; p. 39, Mack Trucks, Inc.; p. 40, Paul W. Hatmon.

Superwheels & Thrill Sports

Lerner Publications Company
241 First Avenue North, Minneapolis, Minnesota 55401